Grief Journal For Kids:

Navigating Storms of Grief for 6-10 year olds

Grief is like a storm—intense, unpredictable, but also a natural part of life. This journal is a space for you to express yourself, reflect, and find moments of calm amidst the chaos. Remember: It's okay to feel everything. There's no 'right' way to grieve, only your way.

ANNETTEATHY.COM | © 2024 ANNETTE ATHY, LLC

Welcome to your Navigating Storms of Grief Journal!

This journal was created just for you to help you understand and share your feelings as you go through this tough time. There's no right or wrong way to use this journal—just be yourself!

Here's How to Get Started:

1. Pick a Page: Start wherever you want—there's no need to go in order. Flip through the pages and choose the question or activity that feels right for you.
2. Express Yourself: Write, draw, or color your feelings. Use words or pictures—whatever helps you share your thoughts best.
3. Ask for Help (If You Want): You can do this journal on your own, or ask a grown-up to help if you'd like to talk about your answers together.
4. Take Your Time: You don't have to finish it all at once. Go at your own pace, and come back whenever you need.
5. Use the Extra Pages: There are blank pages for you to scribble, doodle, or draw anything you're feeling—let your creativity shine!

A Few Things to Remember:

- It's okay to feel sad, angry, confused, or even happy sometimes. All your feelings are important.
- This journal is your space—it's for you to explore your thoughts and feelings in a way that feels comfortable.
- Every storm passes, and with time, you'll find your way through.

We're so proud of you for taking this step to understand and share your feelings. You're stronger than you know! 💕

With care,

Dr. Annette Athy

Discover Your Grief Storm™ Type

Take the Grief Storm™ Quiz to uncover how grief shows up for you. Learn more about your emotions and find tools to help you navigate them.
griefstormquiz.com

Dr. Annette Athy
Grief Coach & Consultant
ANNETTEATHY.COM

Part 1: understanding My Grief Storm™ Type

With your grown-up's permission, discover your Grief Storm type, take a moment to reflect in your journal—do you agree with your type? Why or why not? griefstormquiz.com

What does your storm of grief feel like in your body? Draw or write about it.

_____

_____

_____

_____

_____

_____

_____

_____

_____

_____

_____

_____

_____

_____

_____

_____

_____

_____

_____

_____

_____

_____

_____

_____

_____

If your storm of grief had a color, what would it be? Can you draw it?

Life Reclaimed

What are three words to describe how you're feeling today?

Is there something about the person who died that you really miss? Draw or write about it.

_____

_____

_____

_____

_____

_____

_____

_____

_____

_____

_____

_____

_____

_____

_____

_____

_____

_____

_____

_____

If your feelings were an animal, what animal would they be today? Draw it!

Life Reclaimed

What helps you feel a little better when you're sad?

Think of a happy memory with your loved one? Write or draw it!

Life Reclaimed

Life Reclaimed

What questions do you have about what happened?

_____

_____

_____

_____

_____

_____

_____

_____

_____

_____

_____

_____

_____

_____

_____

_____

_____

_____

_____

_____

Write or draw a picture of your grief storm™ type as weather (rain, lightning, clouds).

Life Reclaimed

What do you think your loved one would say if they could see you right now?

Life Reclaimed

Are there times when your storm of grief feels smaller? What are you doing during those times?

_____

_____

_____

_____

_____

_____

_____

_____

_____

_____

_____

_____

_____

_____

_____

_____

_____

_____

Life Reclaimed

Who helps you feel safe or happy when you're sad?

Life Reclaimed

What's something that makes you smile? Draw it!

Life Reclaimed

Life Reclaimed

If you could ask your loved one anything, what would it be?

_____

_____

_____

_____

_____

_____

_____

_____

_____

_____

_____

_____

_____

_____

_____

_____

_____

_____

_____

_____

_____

_____

How does your body feel when you're sad or angry?

Imagine you're holding a balloon filled with your sadness. What happens when you let it go?

_____

_____

_____

_____

_____

_____

_____

_____

_____

_____

_____

_____

_____

_____

_____

_____

_____

_____

_____

_____

_____

_____

_____

What's your favorite memory with your loved one?

Life Reclaimed

If your grief had a sound, what would it be?
Can you describe or draw it?

Life Reclaimed

Life Reclaimed

Is there something you wish other people understood about your grief storm™ type?

Discover Your Grief Storm™ Type: griefstormquiz.com

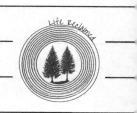

What helps your heart feel calm?

Life Reclaimed

Part 2: Remembering My Loved One

What was your favorite thing to do with your loved one?

Draw or write about a special day you spent with them.

What was their favorite food?
Have you eaten it since they died?

Life Reclaimed

If you could give them a present, what would it be? Draw or describe it.

Life Reclaimed

What's something your loved one taught you?

Life Reclaimed

Draw a picture of your loved one.

What was something they always said to you?

Write them a letter.

What do you think they would want you to know about them?

Life Reclaimed

Think of a smell, song, or sound that reminds you of them?

Life Reclaimed

What was their favorite holiday? How can you celebrate it in their memory?

Life Reclaimed

If your loved one was an animal, what kind would they be? Draw it!

Is there a way you could make something special to remember them? What would it be?

_____

_____

_____

_____

_____

_____

_____

_____

_____

_____

_____

_____

_____

_____

_____

_____

_____

_____

_____

_____

Life Reclaimed

What do you miss most about them?

If you could tell them one thing, what would it be?

What made your loved one laugh?
Draw or write about it.

Life Reclaimed

What's a story you've heard about them that you really like?

(lined writing space)

What made your loved one unique or special?

Life Reclaimed

Do you have something that belonged to them? How does it make you feel?

Life Reclaimed

Imagine your loved one is sending you a hug. How does it feel?

_____

_____

_____

_____

_____

_____

_____

_____

_____

_____

_____

_____

_____

_____

_____

_____

_____

_____

_____

_____

_____

_____

_____

_____

Life Reclaimed

Part 3: Exploring My Feelings
Draw or write about what makes you happy?

What do you do when you feel angry?

Life Reclaimed

Is it hard to talk about your feelings?
Why or why not?

Draw what it feels like to cry.

What do you do when you feel scared?

Life Reclaimed

Draw a picture of yourself feeling calm. What helps you feel that way?

What do you do when you feel lonely?

Life Reclaimed

Who can you talk to when your feelings feel big?

Life Reclaimed

If your feelings were a roller coaster, what would the ride look like?

Do you think it's okay to feel sad and happy at the same time? Why?

_____

_____

_____

_____

_____

_____

_____

_____

_____

_____

_____

_____

_____

_____

_____

_____

_____

_____

When was the last time you felt really loved?

Draw a picture of a time you felt
angry or confused.

What makes you feel better after a hard day?

Life Reclaimed

Think of a time when you laughed really hard?
Draw or write about it.

Life Reclaimed

Life Reclaimed

What does love feel like to you?

If your feelings were a color today, what color would they be?

_____

_____

_____

_____

_____

_____

_____

_____

_____

_____

_____

_____

_____

_____

_____

_____

_____

_____

_____

_____

Life Reclaimed

What's something you're afraid of?

Who helps you feel brave?

Is it okay to be sad forever? Why or why not?

Life Reclaimed

What's one thing you can do to feel a little better when you're upset?

Life Reclaimed

Part 4: Building My Grief Toolbox
What's one thing you can do to help your storm of grief feel smaller?

Who do you trust to share your feelings with?

Life Reclaimed

What's a song that makes you feel calm or happy?

Draw or write about your safe place.

What's something kind you can do for yourself today?

_____

_____

_____

_____

_____

_____

_____

_____

_____

_____

_____

_____

_____

_____

_____

_____

_____

_____

_____

_____

_____

_____

Imagine blowing out a candle for every big feeling. Can you draw it?

Who in your life makes you feel loved and supported?

_____

_____

_____

_____

_____

_____

_____

_____

_____

_____

_____

_____

_____

_____

_____

_____

_____

_____

_____

_____

_____

_____

If you could build a "grief toolkit," what would you put in it?

What's one thing that helps you feel peaceful?

Life Reclaimed

Is there a special place that reminds you of your loved one?

_____

_____

_____

_____

_____

_____

_____

_____

_____

_____

_____

_____

_____

_____

_____

_____

_____

_____

_____

_____

_____

_____

What's your favorite way to relax?

Life Reclaimed

Who is someone you can call or talk to when you feel sad?

_____

_____

_____

_____

_____

_____

_____

_____

_____

_____

_____

_____

_____

_____

_____

_____

_____

_____

_____

_____

Draw a big heart and fill it with things that make you happy.

Imagine your grief storm™ type as a kite. What helps you fly it higher or bring it back down?

_____

_____

_____

_____

_____

_____

_____

_____

_____

_____

_____

_____

_____

_____

_____

_____

_____

_____

_____

_____

_____

Life Reclaimed

What does being brave mean to you?

What's a kind thing someone has done for you recently?

What's one small thing you can do to feel stronger?

_____

_____

_____

_____

_____

_____

_____

_____

_____

_____

_____

_____

_____

_____

_____

_____

_____

_____

_____

_____

_____

_____

_____

_____

_____

If you had a magic wand, what would you wish for right now?

How do you show someone you care about them?

Life Reclaimed

Imagine planting a garden for your loved one. What flowers would you grow?

Life Reclaimed

Part 5: Looking Forward
What's one thing you're excited about?

What's something you've learned about your grief storm™ type?

Discover Your Grief Storm™ Type: griefstormquiz.com

What would you like to remember about your loved one forever?

_____

_____

_____

_____

_____

_____

_____

_____

_____

_____

_____

_____

_____

_____

_____

_____

_____

_____

_____

_____

_____

_____

_____

_____

_____

If your loved one could send you one message, what do you think it would be?

Life Reclaimed

What's something you've done recently that made you proud?

Write about a way to help someone else feel better.

What's a dream or goal you have for the future?

Life Reclaimed

Imagine a rainbow after your storm of grief.
What's at the end of it?

_____

_____

_____

_____

_____

_____

_____

_____

_____

_____

_____

_____

_____

_____

_____

_____

_____

_____

_____

_____

_____

_____

Life Reclaimed

What do you think your loved one would say about how you're doing now?

_____

_____

_____

_____

_____

_____

_____

_____

_____

_____

_____

_____

_____

_____

_____

_____

_____

_____

_____

_____

_____

What's a way you can honor your loved one in the future?

Life Reclaimed

Who do you want to share happy memories with?

Life Reclaimed

Write about or draw a picture of something you hope for.

Life Reclaimed

What's a new thing you've tried or learned since your loved one died?

Life Reclaimed

If your loved one could visit you in a dream, what would you talk about?

_____
_____
_____
_____
_____
_____
_____
_____
_____
_____
_____
_____
_____
_____
_____
_____
_____
_____
_____
_____
_____
_____

Life Reclaimed

What's one thing you've done to feel brave recently?

_____

_____

_____

_____

_____

_____

_____

_____

_____

_____

_____

_____

_____

_____

_____

_____

_____

_____

_____

_____

_____

_____

Life Reclaimed

Imagine sending a letter to your loved one in the sky. What would it say?

_____

_____

_____

_____

_____

_____

_____

_____

_____

_____

_____

_____

_____

_____

_____

_____

_____

_____

_____

_____

_____

_____

What makes you feel hopeful?

What's something you're curious about or want to learn?

If you had three wishes, what would you wish for?

_____

_____

_____

_____

_____

_____

_____

_____

_____

_____

_____

_____

_____

_____

_____

_____

_____

_____

_____

_____

_____

How can you keep your loved one's memory alive in your heart?

Life Reclaimed

Made in the USA
Las Vegas, NV
09 January 2025

16147867R00069